Content Performance Philosophy

When it comes to content, let's be honest: It's never been harder. We expect content to do something for our businesses. We want it to drive results – directly or indirectly.

Content performance cultures were not a thing when I started in print journalism. Content performed when your boss liked your articles and nobody complained about them.

In my third book on content strategies I will share the latest steps that I've seen work and that can be implemented by many teams when they put their minds to them. I also will cover some of the latest business storytelling strategies – including podcasting and artificial intelligence.

Today, content must show ROI of some kind. So how do we get there or at least have a chance? My 5 pillars of a content performance culture can help you get on the right track. The pillars are:

- An embraced content performance culture
- Innovation by all
- Next play mentality
- Right players in the right seats
- Ongoing evaluation

Before we dive into setting up a team, let's define what business storytelling even is and how it helps brands differentiate.

What is business storytelling?

Business storytelling is the art and science of sharing your company's stories. Think of how salespersons hop on calls. They tell the relevant pieces of the company's story. "Oh, that's the problem you are trying to address? We created xyz because of abc to address that."

What stories we share specifically depends on where in the customer journey the consumer is.

- At the top of the funnel, we might share thought leadership content and discuss topics they care about. Podcasts fit here, too.

- Towards the middle of the funnel, it might be how-to content.
- At the bottom of the funnel, when people are ready to buy, it might be more about the features of a product and the story behind why they exist, and how they can help you.

Business storytelling is the art and science of having a straightforward brand story that helps your company position itself in the market and keeps the audience at the forefront.

How do you know what your business story is?

Businesses started for one reason or another. Start there. Ask the founders why the company started. What prompted it? Are there specific problems that appeared that accelerated the company launch?

This can be a good foundation for telling the business story in the future. But sometimes, founders will say things like they stumbled into the business or took it over from somebody retiring or leaving for another reason.

While these are perhaps interesting personal anecdotes, the value to the customer of knowing those stories is probably not that high.
Use what you have when it makes sense and share it with customers when it's relevant. But ask deeper questions:

- Why would our customers care about this?
- How do we know?
- What do we have to say that is likely unique about us?
- How will we share this content, and how will it be produced?

Keep in mind that the stories we share also must be believable. We can't just say that we are good at this or that when we are not. The service, product, and story, after all, have to align.

The channels

The number of channels indeed has exploded in recent years. I recommend using the Create Once, Publish Everywhere Model (COPE) to get the most out of your business storytelling. And the features of all the different channels change, too.

As a general rule, I would recommend focusing on:

- Building your home base on your website
- Hop on trending new social media features quickly to see if they can drive quick wins. That could include web stories, TikTok trends, and even livestreams with experts.
- Use the right mix of paid and organic strategies to drive shorter-term and long-term engagement.

Keep in mind that some channels move quickly (like paid) while others (think SEO) might take a while to drive results. The trick is to have an integrated business storytelling strategy and keep going.

It's also often okay to repurpose content across channels. Sometimes that's in full and at other times it could be pieces of other content assets.

The emotion

Our stories need to bring out an emotion in our audience. They can't just be corporate gobblygook.

People connect around emotions, Ashley Poynter, of Content Rewired explained on my podcast. That could be fear, happiness or sadness.

"Empathize with your audience," she said. "Instead of just talking at them."

Some B2B brands or their leaders have grown up in the age of where businesses do *serious* marketing. That's okay to an extend, but can also be overdone. And hinder brands from standing out.

Sometimes it's about lengthy and unnecessary workflows and approval processes.

Why does this person and this one and that one and five more get to edit every piece of content? Do they have any experience in editing? Do they know what keywords we are trying to rank for? I've seen "editors" edit the important stuff out because they are editing for personal preference, too.

Sometimes it's as simple as using more creative words. For example, a podcast host of a show for accountants might say "Why don't you stop crunching numbers for a minute and crunch our subscribe button."

Ashley recommends that expectations should be set for everyone who is involved in the process. What's their role? What's the expectation of what they can and cannot do. People involved must understand the importance of emotion in the marketing strategy.

As they say, action can beat inaction, and the same is true when it comes to the time when we create a content marketing strategy. But what are the steps to take to move the idea and concept of our content into reality? So let's dive into that topic.

It won't do us any good if it's not implemented. Using the content operations framework can help teams implement more successfully.

1. Set up content operations

Content operations refer to the setup in a company of a content team, its workflows, and processes. Therefore, setting up the proper content ops framework is essential as it can help us implement content strategy correctly.

It defines:

- Roles and responsibilities, including who edits and approves what
- Timelines
- Workflows and steps to take in projects to implement content strategy
- Commitments to content output and results

2. Starting with the strategy

Indeed, we need to start here, and we should document the strategy even if it's at a high level.

We want to start thinking about how we implement our culture of strategic writing - or content creation in general. First, determine your story, the topics you should cover on your various channels for your target audience, and define workflows to share stories so that they are most meaningful to your audience.

First, we need to determine the centerpiece content asset of our strategy. This could be your blog, your webinars, or your podcast. My blog is my centerpiece content asset, but a lot of the content is inspired and draws from the range discussed on my Business Storytelling Show Podcast.

So, while my No. 1 goal is to grow the blog, the email list, and so forth, that might not be possible without running a successful podcast that reaches an audio audience and enables me to create better content.

3. Determining the workflow

As a next step, we have to determine and agree upon the workflow, which includes addressing who does what and the frequency of content. For example, that can include:

- 1-3 livestreams and podcasts per week
- 1-2 in-depth blog posts per week
- 1-4 optimized and updated content pieces that already exist

From there, determine how these items are created. What platform to use for the live stream and podcast? I use Restream and then publish my podcast to all the podcast networks.

I prefer to create directly in WordPress, and editing can happen there. However, even if you can't follow the write-in-WordPress process, have a collaborative discussion about what techniques and tools should be used.

Making the time

Making time for writing can be a challenge. So how do we find it or make it with meetings after meetings, Slack messages piling up, and other interruptions?I share some of my favorite tips and some of the things that work for me.

Making it a priority

It comes down to making the time, making sure others understand that we are writing, and then sticking to the plan. Of course, I realize that's easier said than done, so let's dive into some tips.

But, do keep in mind: You have to decide that writing is a priority or even these steps won't work.

Blocking time

I'm a big fan of blocking time to make time for writing or any task. So my calendar looks like this:

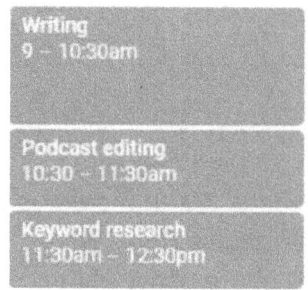

Sometimes, things move ahead, or I skip ahead to a task. For example, if I need a break from writing, I might fiddle with a podcast for a bit next. But in general, blocking off time is helpful.

I also try to batch things as much as possible:
- Writing in one big chunk or maybe even a whole day
- Meetings on another day

Batching by day isn't always possible for some teams, but the more I can batch related tasks, the more productive I seem to be.

Plan realistically

While planning, be realistic about what can get done in a given amount of time. For example, I know roughly how long it will take me to write a decent blog post if I have the source material ready.

Give yourself some cushion. Also, don't let the calendar put unnecessary pressure on you. For example, I've seen people say things like this before:

Let's work as hard and fast as we can for 90 minutes, and then we are done. That might work if you create widgets, but it doesn't necessarily work in the creative world of writing. So, yes, deadlines can be helpful, but only if they are reasonable.

Starting small

Author Marc Reklau talks about starting small. Do the tasks that can be quick wins first, especially when trying to change a habit. It's much easier to write 100 words each morning than 1,000, for example, to get started.

Prioritize what works

Some content will perform better than others. And while it can be a guessing game at times, do try to create more of what has been working and less of what isn't.

For example, I've had a ton of success with Amazon product review videos on the video content side of things.

You may find similar higher-value content pieces in your writing or even the type of writing. For example, once I see a trend of something working in an email campaign, I try to follow that style. I'm not investing more time into email now, but I'm going about what I'm creating differently.

4. Accountability

To keep going is an essential component of a successful content marketing strategy. That's where the importance of accountability comes in.

Using the right technology can also help us be accountable to ourselves and our teams. I know that I pay attention when Trello pings me to let me know a task is due soon. You can also easily pull up the checklists in meetings to see where bottlenecks exist and where other team members might be able to help.

Holly Adams offers an accountability worksheet on her website.

Creating the culture to make it work

To make it work, it is essential to have the right culture. For example, don't tell the public how you collaboratively created a product if collaboration isn't encouraged in the company.

Creating a culture that publishes good business stories only works when content is actually published. This does seem like common sense, but some teams can overthink or over-engineer the publishing part. That can include way too many approvers for each piece of content: slow production times and even siloed teams.

Workflows should be as easy as possible with the proper checks and balances. Yes, content should be reviewed, but we need to accomplish that somewhat efficiently.

The same holds for production. I'm not a fan of content being created on one platform, then copied and pasted into another where it gets published. Those workflows, which admittedly were very common and still are to an extent, add time and the possibility of adding mistakes.

It's also useful for executives to lend their brands in business storytelling. Share stories on social media, publish guest articles, and more. Of course, that doesn't mean the execs have to do all the work – get help from marketing! But being out there helps.

Also, consider the importance of internal communications. Share updates with employees that can easily be consumed. Maybe an internal podcast is a way to go. Or soundbite – but more frequent – updates in Slack channels.

When teams share content publicly, make sure it's somehow shared internally.

Using the right technology

Technology doesn't create culture, but it certainly can enable it. That's why it's so important to use the right tools that don't slow us down, that are easy to use, and help us succeed with our business storytelling. Here are some of the software platforms that I use for content production.

- WordPress for article production and publishing. Easy to use and allows all article assets to be in one place.
  - Yoast SEO Plugin. The Yoast plugin gives me an instant grade on my writing for SEO and readability.
  - Grammarly. Grammarly gives me further editing and writing grades and tips while working on the content. It directly integrates with WordPress through the Grammarly plugin.
- Restream. I use Restream to multistream my live-streamed podcast and record it for my audio podcast.

- Trello. To keep track of projects.
- Canva. Some design work.
- Copylime. AI headline recommendations.

My point here is: To make business storytelling a success, find a way to publish those stories.

An Embraced Culture

Content performs when content teams know:

- their personas
- the best syndication channels
- keep producing content that the target audience wants to consume

Content can perform when you know what the goal should be. This could range from:

- Communication success for internal communications measured by feedback
- Pageviews for content publishers
- New and more users on product sites

- Content that drives SEO to get product pages to rank

At the very least leadership and teams need to be clear what the goals are and are able to brainstorm on ways to reach them.

And then the teams go after their goals on the right interval.

Of course, having a content performance culture does mean that we're looking at performance. Are articles performing or are they not?

On the flipside, the analytics game is still very fractured. There's so many tools and so many ways to measure. I hear marketers complain all the time about measurements:

- Too many measurements
- Too many platforms
- Those measurements are not what we want

And yes, ultimately all content actions at some point need to help with revenue –

directly or indirectly. Content marketing does that.

Content marketing friend Andy Crestodina goes as far as saying that content marketing and blogging doesn't drive many leads but actually helps rank other pages – the pages with products that make money! – rank better. He's got a point.

He also told me on my Business Storytelling Show that his company drives revenue by sharing highly valuable and deep content every two weeks. Media Orbit Studios creates websites for companies, a service they need every three years. So staying top of mind to them and at the right time is highly important. The two-week interval seems to do the trick, according to Andy.

Innovation by All

Another pillar of a content performance culture is innovation by all.

Innovation comes in many forms and really every role on a team can be innovative on its own level.

Front line staff can catch workflows that need to be updated with a new strategy in mind.

I'm thankful when a front line employee told me about an issue with a stated strategy. It was something I would've never known without getting the word from somebody who was working on it daily.

Managers can keep looking for bottlenecks and other issues in implementation of a strategy as well.

Executive sponsors can push new innovative technologies and allow team members to try new things. Of course, they can be as clear as possible about a stated strategy and open to questions and discussions.

Strategies don't just come from the top in a truly matrixed innovative model. I would recommend having some kind of matrix organization that allows cross-team accountability. So people are not just reporting to one person even though they have a manager but they also are accountable to other project leads.

Everyone can share ideas AND build on each other. Pixar and Disney have called this plussing.

- Idea is presented
- Others build on it. Or at least try.

Not all ideas are good ones and some initial ideas that are terrible turn into winners once they are verbalized and plussed.

Sure, innovation should happen within an overarching strategy and framework, but everyone can participate and should do so.

Share what you think can help a content and marketing team move forward and drive content performance toward company goals.

Holly Adams asked an interesting question over on her blog at hollyadamsconsulting.com: Do you think to talk or talk to think?

Good question and I would say I fall into the talk to think category.

I actually think that helps me collaborate. I learn and uncover out loud.

Sure, sometimes people will pick on it and push back on something they thought they heard. I was talking to think, though, I did put thought into it as well.

Questions certainly can show your bias and agenda, but they are also tools we use to gather details and then form next steps.

Some people call that wishy washy but it's just one of several different styles.

The other – as Holly mentioned – is to think to talk.

The important part here is to know when that's somebody's style.

Also it's interesting that generations of children have been told to "think before you speak."

That's good advice and thinking about the words we are going to say is important. I do that too but I don't let it stop me from talking to think - i.e. collaborating.

One thing I love about talking to learn is that you aren't always looking to say "the right" thing.

It's about moving the conversation forward and learning. It actually helps teams enjoy the journey-and most importantly build on it. It's one way to create the content performance culture.

The trick of collaboratively communication is that people in a group should try to understand:

- their own style
- the impact it has on others
- the style of others
- how those styles mesh - or don't
- how to work through the differences
- how the conversation helps us move toward a business goal

Different styles are okay and it's super helpful to understand and work with them. Of course that's a two-way street for all involved.

Innovation also includes trying different techniques and strategies. That could include some of the emerging strategies of:

Text-to-speech content

Providing a text-to-speech content option on your website is another way to make content consumption and engagement easy for web visitors. But, how does text-to-speech work? And how does it fit into our content workflow?

What is text-to-speech on a website?

Text-to-speech on a website usually involves a player directly included on a webpage. People can then click and play the audio to listen to what was written in the text on that page in that player.

Here's an example from the Washington Post, which has computer-generated audio reading many of its articles.

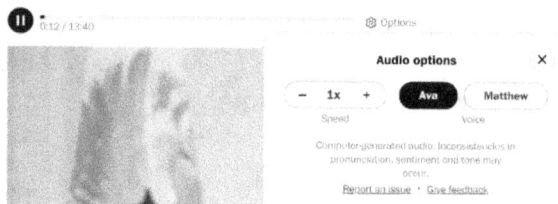

You can pick a female or male voice to read the article to you and can even adjust the reading speed. I'm a bit of a news junky, and this is a great way to get even more out of my digital subscription.

Corporate websites – especially the ones that share content worth consuming – can certainly use this strategy to offer content in different ways.

The sound of computer-generated voices has improved over the years—for example, the voices on the Washington Post sound close enough to my ear to humans. On the flip side, I've listened to podcasts before and thought it was a computer-generated voice and didn't like the experience there.

I suppose it can be about the expectation. On the Post site, I expect the voices to not be from an actual person, but on the podcast, I wasn't expecting that, and there was no mention that it was before the show started.

Ron Jaworski, CEO of Trinity Audio, which provides an AI player for this strategy, said that some consumers could be more likely to listen to content than read it. They can do that while doing other things.

Ron said text-to-speech can help with accessibility.

How to implement text-to-speech

There are a couple of ways to implement a text-to-speech strategy. First, you can undoubtedly record yourself reading your articles on the true do-it-yourself side. I do that from time to time and then publish the audio as a podcast and embed that episode on the website.

You can also use third-party tools like Trinity Audio to add a player that automatically creates the audio for the webpage.

Ron also explained that you could grab the audio from the player and publish it as a podcast. That's a great way to use the Create Once, Publish Everywhere model, especially if you currently don't have a podcast. I would recommend having a note at the show's beginning like: "This episode's audio was auto-generated from an article on <website name.>."

What teams benefit the most from text-to-speech automation?

Content teams that create a lot of written content can stand to drive the most significant advantage from this strategy. They already have a ton of written content, and this strategy could easily repurpose that written content into audio content – including podcast episodes.

Given that this process can be automated, it shouldn't add ongoing work to content creators and strategists. That's certainly always a good thing.

Trends

Innovative teams also hop on trends. That can include TikTok trends. And now younger generations use TikTok as their search engine so there's value in being there and also sharing content that can be found.

Constant change

Things are constantly changing. I hope that's not a debate anymore at this stage, but how can we stay ahead of change and maybe even predict the future of marketing to an extent?
Futurist Rebecca Costa joined me on an episode of the Business Storytelling Show to discuss the future of marketing – and anything that affects our lives.

At the core, we have always predicted or tried to predict what will happen in the future.

We predict our boss' reactions, and the better we know them, the more "data" (knowledge) we have to pull from to base our decision on, the more likely we are to make the correct prediction.

That's a simple example that probably many can relate to. And predicting the boss becomes easier the more we understand and know them. The more prior examples of behaviors we can draw on, the easier it becomes to predict anything.

In the case of the future of marketing, that can include understanding:
- where to reach consumers
- what messages resonate with them
- where they are in the current funnel
- what their behaviors are and how they are changing
- how organic and paid strategies are evolving
- And more...

Predicting the future in companies

It is good to acknowledge the difference between knowing vs. predicting. Knowing means we absolutely, 100 percent understand what will happen. Predicting means that we base our analysis of a likely outcome on data and maybe intuition at the correct times.

How to predict the future

Rebecca said that predicting the future has become more accessible in theory.

"We are getting close to 100 percent," she said. "There are signs."

Whether it's business, politics, or professional sports, there's data to pull from to understand what the likely outcome could be.

"But you need to have the mindset," she said. People have to be willing to pay attention, analysis, and consider.

Why Next-Play Mentality Matters

Things change so quickly today. Marketing is complex and it's hard to win when we don't run the next play and test.

I think the trick is this:

- Do your best
- Evaluate
- Try again
- Repeat

Michael Brenner, author of *Mean People Suck*, told me on the Business Storytelling

Show, that many strategies fail in implementation because bosses and leaders are jerks. "The time of smart jerks needs to be over," he said.

Run the next play.

What are Personas?

Personas are used in content marketing to understand our audiences – basically the people we are creating content for. Personas - as HubSpot would say – are semi-fictional personifications of our perfect customers.

The more we know about the people we are producing relevant content for, the easier that content creation can become. We know how to frame the content and what stories to pursue and publish. Because we know them, their preferences and their likes. But there's a fine line...

Personas can help us understand our audience better.

Personas often describe the following as it relates to our audience members:

- Interests
- How they talk to each other and how they likely want to be talked to
- Technology use
- Likely social media networks and other media consumption
- Other relevant information

Personas help content creators and remind them how and where their target audiences can be reached. Most importantly, they help content producers create content that those audience members actually want to consume.

What's Search Engine Optimization (SEO)?

No matter where you are seeing success, building your website is essential and that includes SEO optimization.

SEO is when we create content with what people are searching for in mind. For example, if people search for content marketing storytelling but not authentic storytelling why would I ever write about authentic storytelling? I should refocus the content to content marketing storytelling.

Sometimes new content is ahead of the search engine volume. For example, when Nike released the Colin Kaepernick commercial, that drove searches for the brand and ultimately sales, too. Keep in mind that 15 percent of all searches on Google each day have never been searched before. So there's room to hit those in your SEO strategy – accidental or not. Of course, it's a bit of a guessing game. You can use Google Trends to find ideas.

At the most basic level, SEO means that we keep in mind what people search for and what terms they use in their searches while we create our content.

Common Current State

Let's say you create content, are a decent journalistic storyteller, and share somewhat in-depth solutions and ideas in your content. At some point, one of your articles will show up in search engine searches.

I've seen it happen over and over and over.

Sometimes the articles that rank aren't the ones we want to rank the most. I say "the most" because if we didn't want it to succeed why did we even write it?

They may not attract the audience we are actually trying to go after. But because people are searching for the topic and we have an in-depth article that appears to answer the question so we rank.

Some people throw their hands up and argue that SEO doesn't work. The strategy – the one they didn't have to begin with – isn't working. <Face palm>. Of course, they aren't totally wrong. We are reaching a different audience. A new one. Maybe even the wrong one. But audiences also evolve.

Congratulations, you can write articles that rank without a strategy. It's kind of like saying I can throw a football without a game plan. I can and sometimes I may even throw a touchdown… in the flag football game in my in-laws backyard. But I'm not going to make it to the NFL on that.

So there's a reason to take it up a notch and also look at what we can learn from the existing content and how we can maximize it.

Right Players

Certainly, there are some standard roles that content teams should have. Every team needs people who can write and who can write the right kind of content.

As they say, great teams are made up of members that complement each other. Sometimes, teams have the right people but they aren't always in the right seats or positions.

Diversity

Building and maintaining diverse teams can make our content and marketing strategy better—no doubt about it. Different backgrounds, life experiences, and skills can round out a team to set us up for better business success.

That's the topic Michelle Ngome, an inclusive marketing expert, and I discussed on an episode of The Business Storytelling Show.

What is a diverse team?

What does a diverse team look like? It's easy to explain what it does not look like. When everyone is the same – think five white guys or really any constellation of people that is the same. That is not a diverse team.

A diverse team should reflect our target market, audience, and society.

How to build a diverse team?

In many cases, there's no geographical boundary to building a content or marketing team. I know some people try to tell you that everyone still has to sit at desks next to each other to work. There certainly is the truth that in-person collaboration can be helpful from time to time.

But, content strategists and marketing ops teams create content, campaigns, and review metrics – among other things. There's no advantage to sitting next to somebody else while doing those tasks. On the other hand, it might even be disadvantageous to have people nearby and be interrupted by unrelated chit-chatter. Working remotely can work.

The awareness and commitment

Like many things, it needs to start with the awareness that you are trying to build a diverse team. That includes looking at the current group. Who is currently on the team? Where are the gaps, and how can we fill them.

Then there needs to be a commitment to building a diverse and high-performing team.

The implementation

Sometimes people will say that they can't hire a more diverse team because the applicant pool is what it is. That's why leaders can't be stuck wanting to hire in just one location.

Expand the geography of where team members can be located.

Also, consider where you are posting openings, Michelle said. For example, publish an opening on the African-American Marketing Association's job board to reach Black marketers.

Consider other places where you might need to advertise or post your opening. Don't forget about networking with groups and others that can make an introduction.

Having a diverse team can make our strategies so much better. The different opinions, thoughts, and ideas can help us be more creative and perhaps be even more efficient at being creative. And, after all, being creative and doing it within the goals of a business can help our companies stand out, which after all is what marketing and content strategy try to accomplish.

Writing as the foundation

Not everyone on the team has to be what we might call a wordsmith, but there's a certain level of importance in using words correctly. That includes really all facets of content - emails, podcasts, blog posts, and more. That includes proper word usage.

What is word usage?

The term word usage refers to the practice of using the best possible words for a specific situation, channel, story, etc. That includes using the most descriptive word that people relate to, putting the words in the best possible order, and using the right amount of words.

Word usage might also include how content is displayed. For example, we do know that most people skim online content. So long paragraphs shouldn't be used. But the following should:

- Bulleted lists
- Sub headlines
- Bolded words
- Active words
- Correct usage
- Images
- Other content that breaks up text – like relevant podcasts. That makes it easier to skim the words for the reader.

How to use words better in your content

Indeed, it's important to follow correct and currently accepted grammar rules. But, to some people's disdain, grammar rules can evolve.

Focus

Rob Reinalda of Word Czar Media and author of "Why Editors Drink" explained that using the best words comes back to focusing and knowing your message.

- What am I trying to say?
- Who is my audience?
- What am I saying that's different from others?
- Are there specific channels that are better for this message? (Should it be a blog article, podcast, Slack update, etc.)

He calls it the "economy of language." Use the right words, but don't use more words than you have to.

"Using 18 words to say what could be said in seven words, they are just wasting the reader's time," he said.

In this book, he extensively discusses the topics of redundancy and bloating in writing. Some content creators feel the need to produce, produce, produce. I do, too, to an extent. After all, content that isn't made can't perform. And then, we have the whole debate of how longer content potentially performs better than shorter content. Some people take that to mean that content needs to be longer, even when they don't have that much to say about the topic.

Understanding creativity

In a content performance culture, we are always looking for results. Results are necessary, but the pendulum may have swung too far from being creative to over-focusing on results only. Plus, creativity can lead to results.

Understand how the creative process works

Many of us have been in meetings where people bring sticky notes, throw snacks on the conference room table and declare that we are all now ready to brainstorm and be creative.

Ready.

Set.

Go.

Unfortunately, that's not the way to be creative, Creativity Expert Adam Morgan explained. Here's how creativity works:

Give the team an idea about what we are trying to accomplish and then offer them time to think about it themselves. Be sure to actually give them time, though!

Sometimes we hear this as a "Bring your ideas to the meeting" directive. But, for it to work we need to be clear about what we are trying to accomplish and give a few more details.

Then make some ideas on your own, Adam explained.

Thinking time

The problem with allowing thinking time is that it doesn't look productive. But it's necessary.

Bring ideas to a meeting

Bring your ideas to a meeting and then build on each other. Maybe vote on the best ones. Consider sleeping on it again.

Now, this isn't an invitation to overthink and overprocess all creative processes. Adam reminds us that some decisions do not need to go through an entire creative process. Just make a decision.

But in larger projects, it's not good to have one meeting and always make a decision right then. As good as checking decisions off our list is, this isn't a way to be creative.

Finding ideas in other niches

Ideas are everywhere around us and one strategy that I love is linking ideas, which Jim Link discusses in his book "Idea-Links."

The book explains the structure of linking ideas from one area to projects in another unrelated field.

By looking at the world and making mental notes of things around us, we can actually implement ideas from unrelated fields and advance our own industry's current state.

The book, for example, mentioned how the Prius gives its driver instant feedback on how much fuel is being used. The book mentions how drivers like this and even try to get more miles per gallons out of their vehicles.

The book talks about how this phenomenon could be used in other industries. For example, in a home: If you keep this light on here's how much the bill will be.

Staffing

Rob mentioned that staffing – especially at newspapers – has been an issue in editing and writing. Some stories were edited two to three times when I worked as a journalist. With fewer editors doing more work, that's not likely to happen.

Many content creators don't even have anyone reading or reviewing their content before it publishes.

The process

That brings me to process, and we may even call it culture.

I like to follow a process like this:
- First, start with the strategy: What are we doing and why?
- Determine the workflow and the roles.

- Understand the personas
- An outline is next
- Start production. However, that may look. I'm currently a fan of interviewing experts on a live-streamed podcast and then producing written content from that interview.
- Review process
- Publish
- Distribute

Use Trello templates or a similar project management tool to have the process outlined. I especially love template cards because they allow me to check things off as I'm doing them. I sometimes add tasks that take seconds but that I'm prone to forget about. For example, updating the feature image on a blog post.

SLAs

HubSpot's Skill-Up Podcast talked about the importance of having defined rules between team members and teams. The example the podcast gave was to have service-level agreements between marketing and sales. Here's how they can look:

- definition of what a marketing qualified lead is
- determination of how many leads should be delivered at any given time. For example, if marketing delivers 1,000 leads but sales can only follow up with 100 what's the point? Marketing should also be aware of the capacity of the sales team.
- general outline of expectations and follow-up between the two

There certainly is the potential danger of over-documenting anything but outlining the expectations between teams and team members can actually be very helpful to make sure we move forward together with accountability and towards driving performance. That is what a content performance culture is all about.

Ongoing evaluation

The set it and forget it strategy is not something I would recommend. Content strategy is so dependent on other companies nowadays. Think Google with search, social media with shrinking organic reach, and even podcast distribution. Video platforms, too. Our content rises and falls based on what those other companies decide and allow. Of course, we can pay for paid promotions but even those have rules.

Ongoing evaluation and strategy can be compared to what we used to call strategic planning every three years or so. But now it should happen more often and on an ongoing basis.

I've done my fair share of strategic planning in content marketing, digital marketing, and organizational storytelling. I believe in it and know strategic planning is an important part of actually implementing the plan. Keep in mind that the best plan is worthless without implementation. Hope you didn't pay an agency a bunch of money and now it sits on the shelf.

Strategic planning has to be deliberate, thought-through, but not overthought, and then with some ground rules:

- Listen like you are wrong
- Debate like you are right
- Discuss ideas
- Check the ego at the door
- Be open to ideas
- Definite next steps
- Verbal agreement and debate

One executive team I worked with required 70 percent agreement. So if there are 10 people, 7 have to agree. The other 3 should debate but once it's voted on they'll walk with the group decision. No hallway kindergarten backstabbing meetings allowed.

When strategic planning misses a certain level of healthy debate that's not a reason for a pizza party. Of course, debate can be hard in North American business culture, but if it doesn't happen in the planning and ongoing evolution process, how do we know we are pushing innovation?

In years of projects, people like to remind me that innovation and change doesn't always feel good. Same often goes for debate. So it seems like the two go hand in hand!

I asked around on Twitter.

Twitter connection Brian McTague said the following:

"I believe positive debate generates positive conflicts which sparks positive thinking (which generates substantive ideas, not shallow thinking)."

"Business is meant to be a little messy. Debate cleans it up," he said. "A good healthy debate deepens understanding within all involved, increases engagement, spreads ownership."

Of course, when relationships are hurting and people don't trust or at least respect each other, debate is hard. Maybe impossible.

Sometimes people just fall into their habit of agreeing OR arguing. Not because one or the other is better, but that's their default.

"The challenge is that most people either just agree, or simply debate for the sake of debate. The debate should be a thoughtful, brainstorming, exercising and sharing of ideas, " said Jennifer Radke on Twitter.

The absence of debate might also mean that:

The debates are happening in the meeting after the meeting. We aren't pushing the innovation envelope enough.

Sure, we don't want to throw everything out the window. Keep what works and has a chance of continued success.

But if my strategic plan is to do what we did last year, except we will do it this year, why did you just pay the big bucks for strategic planning? Things change quickly in digital marketing and ongoing evaluation can help teams stay ahead of the curve.

We want the right mix of keeping what works, sharing ideas to discuss and then we should try at least some of those ideas.

It's hard. Sure. Here's my counterpoint even: One of my first digital transformation and content marketing change projects, one department was openly opposing many steps of the way.

I thought they were so difficult. And they kind of were. But many of their points were valid and deserved to be worked through. Sometimes that's doable in the current meeting, or we need another meeting and another. Just keep in mind that a decision has to be made at some point. Consider whether it's a debate to collaborate or a debate to stall.

Sometimes we have to sleep on it – a highly underused tactic, by the way.

But if we don't have some pushback we aren't doing something unique or innovative.

I use this checklist to always be open to new ideas and to offer my input:

- Be aware of toxic relationships and try to check them
- Be aware of your trigger words (aka pet peeves) and don't react negatively to them
- Think about it
- Listen!

Especially for leaders the last one is important. You won't get feedback or debate if you never stop talking. Of course, people could also take the liberty to interrupt but you know how that often doesn't happen.

Debate is good and the best leaders love to be proven wrong. I think of "being proven wrong" in a collaborative way as learning.

Have a strategy

Using a good content strategy is another pillar of a content performance culture. They change and often quickly. Keep an eye on them and adjust things on the fly. This is one reason why I typically would recommend to have at least one good strategist on any team. Somebody has to somewhat keep up with all the changes.

Google Search Console is one way to keep track. Google Analytics is another.

With a good strategy everything we do is highly deliberate and for the most part we try to take opinion out of it. One way where that becomes apparent is when it comes to editing.

Your homebase - the website

Any good content strategy and content performance culture needs a homebase. That homebase in many places should be your website. But how do you start?

Always put the consumer first in all your content. Why would they care about this?

"There are a lot of ways to build credibility online," Author John Weiler said. "There are also different degrees."

The different levels are:

- Starting out
- Expert level
- Influencer level

"A lot of businesses are actually already experts and even when you are just starting out but a lot of them don't know how to communicate that," he said.

Also keep in mind that higher levels take more effort, time, and budget. I do think anyone with topical knowledge can become an influencer, but it takes practice, grit, and tenacity to push forward.

Workflows

Workflows are an ever evolving piece, too. What worked 10 years ago and may have been the best way then may not be the best way today.

Let's take podcasts. Back in the day, they were recorded in studios. That's fine and still happens today. But there are also ways to record them with one app, even with remote people, edit and publish.

Writing can happen on computers, phones, and iPads now. You may be typing on a screen, using voice dictation, or swiping.

Using content to build a brand

Companies, employees and their brands can become leaders by creating content performance cultures. Here's how.

1. Share content

You have to share content around your topic, including:

- on your blog
- your YouTube channel
- write a book – from blog content may work
- participate in social media chats
- conference talks
- really everywhere your target consumers are

One thing to keep in mind when it comes to creating content is that it's hard to write highly unique content if you are isolated. Consider getting out there and finding the stories in the wild where your customers and coworkers are. Of course, today there are plenty of technological tools out there that can help with that.

Talk to sales, customer success, and search your internal knowledge repository of customer feedback. The ways to find that unique content can happen today within the right systems.

2. Get on a schedule

Success is easier when you get on a schedule. Here's what I do:

- Podcast on Monday
- Blog almost daily on weekdays, but once a week is fine too!
- Content for other channels - repurpose and throw it a parade!
- Keep an eye out for next book opportunities
- Speak at conferences

3. Try new content channels

This could include TikTok, Instagram Reels, YouTube Shorts - maybe even Web Stories. Don't forget about AI content creation. How can we make our efforts better and drive more results?

Always look for the new ways where content can drive results now!

4. Keep re-evaluating

The best content performance cultures always evaluate everything. That doesn't mean they give up early, but they always look for opportunities and early signs that something is on the right track.

Promote the good things

Building culture is one thing. Making sure people know the culture exists is another. That's where business storytelling comes in. To market culture is important to attract and keep the right people. Storytelling cultures break down silos - internally and externally. Encourage employees to recognize other employees and their success stories.

Ask them to submit the stories or if they want to share them themselves on social media. We should get their permission BEFORE it's shared publicly.

Encourage employees

Companies should also empower employees to share stories as much as possible:

- Hold virtual sessions for employees that offer tips and tricks on how to share stories on social media channels.
- Ask people to share those good stories. The channels are endless from Glassdoor to Facebook to LinkedIn, you name it.

- Recognize and maybe even reward employees for sharing the best stories. So and so is the head storyteller for the month of March because of this fantastic story recognized and shared.
- Amplify the stories employees share from the organizational accounts.

The last part of amplification is backwards to what many companies do today. Marketing writes up some feel good and marketing jargon filled post and then sends them to employees to share across their own networks.

Encouraging employees to share, can get us better stories that can then help us drive that content performance culture.

FriYays

Another tool is to share good stories internally. I'm a fan of doing FriYays. Every Friday I like to send out a note to the team about great things that have happened.

Some shout-outs were small wins that some companies wouldn't consider recognizing in a note. Others were bigger. Then invite other teammates to add their own shout-outs.

From there, when it makes sense and with permission consider sharing some of the stories publicly.

And how is this helping the company? Sharing positive stories that are authentic help the culture. That's not new. When I've looked for a job, there are some companies I don't apply to because of their public image. Some companies I absolutely want to apply to as their brand is strong and stands for something I want to be associated with.

It's similar when it comes to working with certain brands either as their customer or by providing services to them.

It can help your company project a positive brand image when employees share positive and caring stories. It certainly is okay to have an approval process.

That's the external impact. From an internal perspective, it can help, too. Teammates can feel more positive and happier in the current situation.

Create a styleguide

Good content performance cultures have style guides.

While we don't want to overthink things, creating a styleguide for a growing team is helpful.

A company style guide for content strategy is important because it can help us be clear and add consistency in our corporate marketing and storytelling.

Some style discussions can get heated, Take the Oxford comma. But at the end of the day, it's not about whether you love the comma or not. It's about what makes the story clear to the reader! That also should be the goal of any style guide.

In the digital world, here's where style guides could come in especially essential:
- make content consumption easy to the reader! That means it's skimmable.
- give readers the structure to find the information quickly.

Digital style guides keep readers on track.

In digital marketing, style guides can sometimes make the storytelling more formulaic and that's not bad necessarily:

- Here's where the headline goes. Is it title case, sentence case, or what?
- Copy that is always the same (on my blog, that's the email sign up. Other sites have disclaimers – which I have at the bottom on articles) is in certain spots.
- Then comes the new information or story.
- Some calls to action, maybe.
- The photo is always on the top right.
- There's a subhead every 300 words
- Images break up copy as well.
- Etc.

You don't even have to create your own style guide. Using the AP Stylebook is an easy way to implement a style and then build on that for more nuanced uses of content pieces as necessary.

You can also add your styleguide to Grammarly.

Podcasting

Podcasting is one way to differentiate yourself. I would still recommend to use podcast content in other places, like:

- as live-streams
- as written blog posts
- in email marketing

Sharing content through podcasting can be a differentiator. This section shares my latest tips on how to get in front of audiences and keep them engaged through podcasting.

For my podcast episodes, I usually have a rough outline.

- Determine the overarching topic - preferably one that hasn't been covered on the show.
- Starter questions.
- Outline of flow
  - Talk about topic A
  - Then topic A1, B, etc.
  - Wrap it up with a summary and conclusion

I still recommend and like to go on tangents when the answers warrant it. Be prepared, but also go with the flow.

As one reviewer on Apple Podcasts said the best stories come out of follow-up questions. Good follow-up questions also make the recording feel more like a conversation.

When it's just me talking, shows are usually 8-15 minutes. With a guest, they usually end up at 24.

In both scenarios, I record and livestream directly in Restream, but there are many tools you can use to record your show. I love

How to Open a Podcast Episode

Certainly there are many ways to get your podcast started. Some podcasts simply start with an ad. Some start with music-including mine. Some have a quick overview or a quote from the show.

No matter how you start at some point the host has to say something. I've seen several different ways to get that going. Some hosts say "hey guys" or "hello" or "I'm Christoph Trappe and this is the Business Storytelling Podcast."

There certainly are many ways to get the opening right. One that I am a fan of is to address the audience. For example on the Business Storytelling Podcast I try to remember to say something like this:

"Hello business storytellers and marketers. I am Christoph Trappe and today's show is about ..."

There are a couple of things that are helpful to the podcast host, the guest and also the listeners:

The people on the show remember who the audience is and hopefully use that information to shape their information towards the audience's interest.

Keeping the audience top of mind is certainly a best practice and can help everyone.

It gives new listeners an idea if the show is for them. If a podcast host says "hello accountants.." I know pretty quickly that the podcast is probably not for me.

This is not as black-and-white as it sounds because many topics are for several industries. For example, podcast episodes from my Content Performance Culture Podcast are for really anyone who creates content publicly and also internally. That could include:

- Marketers
- Communication professionals
- Internal communicators
- Public relations practitioners
- Talent acquisition reps who are trying to brand the culture externally
- Journalists who are looking for new tools and strategies
- Executives who are looking for strategic and implementation help

There are probably other subgroups that I could add as you might imagine, but I cannot say all those potential audiences at the beginning of each show. So I pick the most prevalent ones and kind of group everyone into the term business storyteller.

What Podcast Metrics Matter?

What podcast metrics should we look at? There certainly are many theories and opinions on the topic, so why not add mine?

Podcast metrics share how many people listen to or watch our podcast episodes. This can include:

- Listens/downloads on podcast channels
- New subscribers/total subscribers
- The total time they watched/listened
- Overall downloads/listens/views of all episodes
- Audience by country

The biggest problems with podcast metrics

The biggest problem is likely how decentralized metrics currently are. For example, my hosting platform gives me some metrics like:

- Overall listens
- Listens by episode
- Top episodes
- Audience by country breakdown
- Listening platforms

I especially like looking at the top episodes metric as it gives me some ideas about what episodes are taking off. Most recently, an episode on LinkedIn newsletters climbed the charts, showing genuine interest in that topic.

To complicate my episodes' actual performance, I also need to keep in mind that I livestream most episodes. So those metrics come from LinkedIn, YouTube, Amazon, X, and sometimes Facebook.

The show is also shown on the DB&A Television Network, which streams in the United States and is carried by dozens of international TV providers. I keep track of all these numbers in my media kit as much as possible because that's a more accurate reflection of the total audience.

How to decide what metrics matter

What metrics matter – as usual – depends on the goal. Some experts recommend that you look at total downloads/listens for the first 30 days after publication.

Some networks and podcast hosts even track that for you. But given that I have these additional channels not included in a podcast host's dashboard, I find the 30-day metric rule cumbersome.

In addition, most of my podcast episodes have timeless content. The Business Storytelling Show isn't a news podcast. It's a content strategy podcast. And some episodes take off way later than the 30-day window.

Take an LinkedIn newsletter episode. It had some listens early on, then started creeping up into the hundreds, and about two years after it was initially published is closing in on 10,000 listens on podcast channels alone.

So there's long-term value for podcast content as well. Somehow, we need to account for that. So I look at my overall metrics:

- The number of listens in the last 7 days of all episodes
- How the last episodes performed
- What are some highlights from the livestreams?
- Are any new episodes creeping up into the list of the top episodes?

The case for repurposing

Certainly, there's value in keeping an eye on how your podcast and livestream strategy is performing. Are people watching and listening? But, also consider this: What are you doing with the content after the podcast and livestream? For example, I turn many of my episodes into written articles, which perform on their own as well.

Without the podcast episodes, I would have never even gotten this content so there's value in post-podcast metrics as well. I know, right? It's not easy to collate the true impact of a podcast strategy when it's made part of a

truly integrated Create Once, Publish
Everywhere Model.

What's the COPE model?

With the multitude of channels out there, the
Create Once, Publish Everywhere concept
stresses the importance of repurposing
content over multiple channels.

This might include:

- Blog
- Several social media networks
- Newsletter
- Printed materials
- Paid campaigns
- Other (digital) channels that are
  relevant

I prefer the blog as the centerpiece and then
content is reformatted from there.

That doesn't mean that we always link back
to the blog, but that we use the blog content
as a starting point. Sometimes it's cut up as
tweets or an image is shared on Pinterest.
Other times, a summary of the article might
be posted on LinkedIn or in a newsletter. The

key to creating once, publishing everywhere is to find the most effective use of content for all channels.

The emergence of AI

We have a little bit of an arms race going on right now when it comes to artificial intelligence for everything. ChatGPT entered the market, and before we knew it companies were springing up right and left, offering their AI services.

In addition, virtually every software tool started integrating AI into their offerings. In fact, AI integration into software is so widespread at the moment that it will no longer be a differentiator in the near future and even now. It's just an expectation.

AI in content creation is also an important discussion right now, because it impacts how companies work, how they create content, and who creates that content.

What Is AI Content And The Stages To Use It

AI content creation can help us create better content if we use it correctly. In reality, many content teams already use AI anyway. But, there are several levels of AI content creation, or should I call it AI-assisted content creation?

As Tech Influencer Evan Kirstel said on "The Business Storytelling Show," there will be winners and losers in the AI content creation game, but trying the technology early on its lifecycle is essential.

What is AI content creation?

Content can be created by artificial intelligence, and there are several artificial intelligence tools out there that do just that. They have different levels of quality and workflow. For example, Copylime.com has an article writer that produces the content based on an outline and charges you credits as you go.

Then we have tools like ChatGPT that write content based on questions or commands. For example, here I asked:

Please write an intro about Christoph Trappe, the content marketer

It responded with:

Christoph Trappe is a renowned content marketer and thought leader in the marketing industry. He has extensive experience creating and executing successful content strategies for B2B and B2C companies and has helped numerous organizations build their brand and engage their target audience through compelling content. Christoph is known for his innovative and data-driven approach to content marketing and has been recognized for his contributions to the field through numerous awards and speaking engagements.

In a nutshell, AI content creation uses artificial intelligence through a question, directive, or even an outline of what the content should entail. In addition to artificial intelligence writing the content, there are other aspects where artificial intelligence can help content creators in their process.

Those areas include artificial intelligence reviewing the content, improving existing content, and scouring through source materials to find the best content to use.

The AI reviews content

Tools like Grammarly check much of our content work already. I know I have it running nonstop in the background as a Chrome extension. Grammarly uses machine learning and artificial intelligence to learn and make better recommendations. This might be the entry point for many content teams for AI. After all, people have used spellcheck and grammar check for decades. This is just a new and advanced way of doing that.

How many drafts are needed to create good content?

This is such an interesting question, as technology has evolved over the years. I've seen content published on first drafts take off and content with too many drafts that didn't drive any results.

And, of course, AI can help us in the process of checking quality and making suggestions. In general, though, how many drafts content needs isn't always directly tied to content performance. I wish it were as easy to say: Oh yea, more drafts set the content up to be more successful. That's not the case - unfortunately! Or, fortunately, if you are stuck in approval hell.

There's an advantage to going through several versions of content - especially when each review has a different purpose.

In other words, it makes no sense for people to review copy or any content purely on personal preference. "Oh, I prefer that word over this word."

Especially when you want your content to rank in search, be sure to check any opinions on wording against what people **actually** search for.

Even in the self-editing process, it's okay to have multiple versions.

What those multiple versions look like depends on the content creator. For example, some like to write and write and write and then cut content back. I've never been a fan of that process, as it seems time-intensive, but if it works for you, it may take less time.

I prefer to follow this process:

- Start with an idea
- Validate that there's potential interest in our market
- Determine what unique angle I can offer
- Create an outline

- Get quotes from internal and external experts to flush out the content
- Write your first official draft
- Self-edit
- Send to the editor for review
- Finalize content
- Publish and promote on social media, email, and other places.

In essence, I consider that six drafts:

1. outline
2. adding quotes
3. adding transitions and my own thoughts
4. self-edit
5. editor
6. finalize

At times, in the self-editing process, I might also ask AI to give me feedback on an article. A response to a draft of this article looked like this:

Sure, I can give you some feedback on your article.

Overall, I think the article is well-written and informative. You do a good job of explaining the importance of multiple drafts and how they can help to improve the quality of your content.

Here are a few specific things I liked about the article:

You start by acknowledging that there is no one-size-fits-all answer to the question of how many drafts are needed to create good content. This is an important point to make, as it allows your readers to understand that the number of drafts they need will vary depending on the specific content they are creating.

You then go on to discuss the benefits of multiple drafts, such as the ability to catch errors, improve clarity, and make sure the content is relevant to your target audience.

You also provide some specific tips for drafting and redrafting content, such as starting with an outline and getting feedback from others.

Here are a few minor things that I would suggest changing or adding to the article:

In the section on "Importance of Multiple Versions," you could add a sentence or two about how multiple versions can also be helpful for marketing purposes. For example, you could create different versions of the same content for different channels (e.g., a blog post for your website, an infographic for social media, etc.).

In the section on "How Drafts Support the Writing Process," you could mention the importance of taking breaks between drafts. This can help you to come back to the content with fresh eyes and make more objective decisions about what needs to be changed.

In the section on "Understanding the Benefits of Editing and Revising," you could add a few more specific examples of the kinds of errors that can be caught during the editing process. This could help your readers to understand the importance of taking the time to edit their content carefully.

Overall, I think the article is a valuable resource for anyone who wants to learn more about the importance of multiple drafts and how to create high-quality content. I would recommend making the minor changes I mentioned above, but otherwise I think the article is well-written and informative.

I hope this feedback is helpful.

Sure, some content can just be pushed out, but any content can see improvements with another set of eyes. That includes looking at the content from the following perspectives:

- Grammatical and proper usage check
- Strategic: Does the content fit with the content strategy?
- Accuracy: Are the stated facts correct?

- Flow

Some writing professionals will say more drafts are better than fewer drafts, but I think, in general, it depends on the following:

- who is writing the content?
- what the topic is.
- how technical it gets.
- what the content needs to be optimized for - search, for example.

Be clear about the process from the beginning. Who needs to see the content, what are people editing for, and where is the content produced?

I'm a fan of written web content to be produced directly in the CMS whenever possible.

For example, in WordPress, I can see the different versions side by side and also measure the content against best SEO practices with the Yoast Plugin.

Remember that the process can take longer or quicker with writers in different stages of their knowledge of the subject matter. More experienced writers might not need as many drafts and stages as a writer in their first job. But just because there are several drafts, that also doesn't mean an experienced writer (or writer of any experience) is worse of a wordsmith.

It's all about improving the content for the audience and driving results.

AI improves content

Then we have the workflow where artificial intelligence improves the content. Grammarly certainly fits in here. So does the underline headline tool in Copylime. I enter an idea for a headline, and then Copylime gives me five ideas for potentially better headlines.

Using AI to Write a Book or Any Content

Artificial intelligence (AI) tools like ChatGPT have exploded in popularity recently, sparking debates about how to use them responsibly. Can AI act as a crutch for lazy writers or help dedicated authors be more productive? What's the best process for leveraging AI when writing a book? Can you be using AI to write a book? And if so, what's the appropriate way to do that?

I spoke with Gleb Tsipursky, author of "ChatGPT for Thought Leaders and Content Creators: Unlocking the Potential of Generative AI for Innovative and Effective Content Creation," on "The Business Storytelling Show" to get his take. Here are eight tips for using AI to write a book.

Start by Brainstorming with AI

One way AI can help authors is by generating ideas to include in the book. Instead of holding traditional brainstorming sessions, you can simply prompt the AI to suggest potential topics, themes, chapter outlines, and more.

Gleb recommends starting a thread with the AI and keeping the conversation going throughout the writing process.

For example, you may ask it to first suggest some initial ideas for the book. Then after reviewing those and picking the strongest ones, come back to the AI and ask it to expand on a specific concept to include as a chapter.

This allows the AI to continuously refine its understanding of your goals, style, and voice. The more interaction you have, the better it can support you.

Consider your source content

AI has to source its content somewhere. One way to ensure it's good content:

- Feeding other articles that should be included into the system and then asking it to "Please combine these articles into one book chapter on the topic of xyz."
- Voice dictating your thoughts to Otter.ai. Then take the transcript and feed it into Claude AI and ask it to write a book chapter on topic xyz based on the attached transcript.

Use AI to Draft Chapters

Once you have your outline, Gleb suggests having the AI generate chapter drafts. Similar to brainstorming, this should be an iterative process:

1. Prompt the AI to write the first section or chapter.
2. Carefully review the draft, editing and revising parts as needed.
3. Feed the revised section back to the AI. Explain what changes you made and why.
4. Have it write the next section based on your edits.
5. Repeat the process until the chapter is complete.

The key is not to treat the AI drafts as final copy. They still require significant reworking. But by continually providing feedback, you train the AI to produce better results over time.

As Gleb explains, "The crucial thing is that editing after the initial generation, that's what gets and makes the content yours because you made significant revisions."

Fine-Tune the AI to Match Your Style

One risk of leaning too heavily on AI-generated writing is ending up with inconsistent tone and voice. Since the models are trained on vast datasets, their default output may not match your own personal writing voice.

Gleb emphasizes feeding your edits back into the AI during drafting to help align its writing more closely with yours. You can also fine-tune the AI by providing upfront examples of your work.

For instance, before having it write any chapters, you could provide a sample from a previous book or article you authored. Let the AI analyze your writing style. Then tell it to use that as a model when generating the new book.

Double Check for Accuracy

Like anyone - human or robot - AI can and does make mistakes. So it's critical to verify accuracy before publishing any AI-generated text.

Gleb recommends several techniques to catch errors:

- Ask the AI to explain its reasoning step-by-step. Thinking through the logic makes mistakes less likely.
- Don't let it make unsupported claims.
- Request a confidence rating for each statement. Focus on double checking areas where it has low confidence.
- Run the draft through multiple AI tools to compare outputs. Differences may reveal errors.
- Manual review and fact checking, just as you would with a human writer.

AI Should Complement, Not Replace Human Writers

At the end of the day, Gleb cautions against viewing AI as a complete replacement for doing the hard work yourself.

The most successful authors will use AI as a tool to augment their skills, not as a crutch. The technology can help generate ideas faster, speed up drafting through iterations, and align the tone to your personal brand. But you still need to actively develop the content, refine it extensively, and ensure quality control.

Think of AI as your new writing partner, not a shortcut. Approach your book as a collaboration and AI can help accelerate the process meaningfully. But don't hand over the reins entirely.

Protect Your Investment by Establishing Copyright

Since AI models produce text by analyzing patterns from publicly available data, their raw output cannot be copyrighted. That presents a risk for authors choosing to publish AI-generated books.

Without editing the content sufficiently to establish your authorship, someone else could copy the AI-written portions freely without penalty. That undermines your ability to build a consistent brand and earn royalties.

Gleb strongly recommends owning your work by revising AI drafts until they reflect your unique perspective and contribution. Make the ideas and language your own. That makes it legally defensible as your creative work product.

How Much Faster Can You Write with AI?

A common question is how much time AI can save when writing. According to Gleb, answers vary depending on each person's skills.

The iterative process of revising multiple drafts with the AI until you have polished chapters does add up. But it's not a magic bullet. As with any high-quality writing, expect the editing to take as long or longer than the initial drafting.

Be realistic about the time savings. AI may help you get 50-75% of the way there faster by autocompleting sentences or generating new directions to explore. But you'll still need to invest significant effort to craft those drafts into a compelling book.

Jumpstart Your Writing Process with AI

At its best, AI serves as fuel to supercharge your creativity, not a pacifier keeping you complacent. Use it to overcome writer's block and build momentum, not as an excuse to be lazy.

Approach your content with a passion for sharing quality ideas. Let AI handle the busywork so you can focus on the fun, creative aspects of writing.

Master the process and AI can help you become a prolific author and content creator.

But never forget that books represent your perspective. Even with AI assistance, your unique voice and vision must come through clearly to connect with readers. Use the technology wisely to share your one-of-a-kind messages with the world.

Finding the best content in source materials

Another way AI can be used is to comb through existing content to help us find themes or relevant quotes. You can use tools like Otter.ai to accomplish that.

Writing AI prompts

As they say "garbage in, garbage out" and that also holds true when working with artificial intelligence tools to level up your marketing. To make AI useful, we have to be **writing AI prompts that are clear, detailed and know what we want** to get from AI.

That means wishy-washy instructions - like some humans give - don't cut it. Writing AI prompts to prompt useful results from AI requires us to give context, background and ask a good question so the AI even knows what we are after and what we expect from its output.

The Basics: What does it mean to be writing AI prompts?

AI writing prompts are text cues that guide artificial intelligence tools to generate relevant responses. They provide context and direction for the AI to compose coherent output that hopefully can help us create more strategic content.

It's basically the direction humans give the AI on what they want it to do or help with. AI prompts can also be a conversation and build on each other in the same thread.

<u>Here's an example of me asking Perplexity AI questions about myself</u>. The same concept of making it an ongoing conversation can be applied to any interaction with AI.

Who is the content marketer Christoph Trappe

Sources

Christoph Trappe |
Linkedin
linkedin · 1

Christoph's Content
Corner - Christoph Trapp...
christophtrappe · 2

About Christoph Trappe
christophtrappe · 3

Christoph Trappe on
Linkedin: I asked ChatGP...
linkedin · 4

Talking Content Marketing
– With Christoph Trappe ...
co · 5

Christoph Trappe |
Buildings
buildings · 6

Answer

Christoph Trappe is a content marketing strategist and consultant [3] [4] [5]. He has worked across many industries, including healthcare, nonprofits, SaaS, publishing, technology, and professional services [3]. He is a career storyteller who has worked as a journalist and a nonprofit executive [3]. Christoph Trappe is also a renowned thought leader in the marketing industry [4]. He was the former chief content officer at Stamats Communications, the parent company of BUILDINGS [6]. Christoph Trappe helps companies move their marketing and communications from happening to performing [1]. He offers useful content from his content strategy consulting services via email [2].

Can you tell me more about his journalism background?

Sources

Christoph Trappe |
Linkedin
linkedin · 1

Christoph Trappe -
Corridor Business Journal
corridorbusiness · 2

About Christoph Trappe
christophtrappe · 3

Christoph Trappe
Biography | Booking Info...
allamericanspeak... · 4

Christoph Trappe's Profile
| Linkedin, Content...
muckrack · 5

Christoph Trappe on
Scribblelive, industry...
relevance · 6

Answer

Christoph Trappe has a background in journalism. He enrolled at the University of Iowa to earn a degree in journalism and play football, imagining a career as a sportswriter. However, he ended up on the police beat at The Gazette in Cedar Rapids, Iowa [4]. Christoph Trappe has also worked as a journalist for Content Marketing Institute [5]. In his career, he has led teams of journalists, content creators, strategists, and designers to successfully drive results [7] [8].

Interesting. Why did he not work as a sports writer?

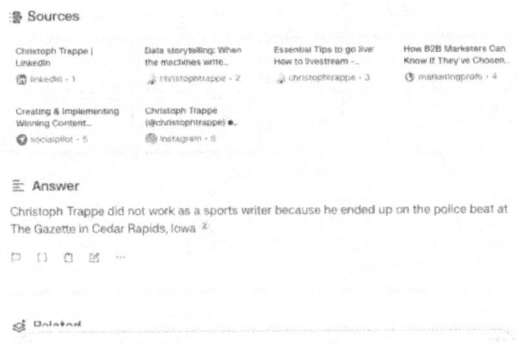

Crafting Effective Prompts

The key to leveraging AI for really anything - but especially to be useful in content strategy - is engineering effective prompts. Here are my top tips:

Be Specific

Give the AI clear direction by explaining exactly what you want it to write about. Avoid vague or generic prompts.

Provide Context

Give the AI some background on the topic and goals to shape the response.

Define Parameters

Not all tools give you different options for output, but if you want a bulleted list, just say that.

Give examples

If you have something comparable already, share that as an example.

Iterate and Optimize

Treat prompts as a work in progress, tweaking and refining them over time.

Provide source content

Give the AI as much information as possible. For example, if I want it to analyze my Search traffic, I could just upload my Google Search Console data to give the AI more background.

Use software that has integrated prompts

Consider using AI tools that have specific functions (aka they have built-in prompts). On the content creation side that includes:

- Copylime has automatic prompts for headlines, outlines, etc.
- Opus Clips automatically creates short videos from longer-form videos

In Opus Clips, you can give some pre-determined prompts like how long a clip should be, the framing, etc. But you can't say: Find me clips that talk about x.

What's important to keep in mind here is that as new tools enter the market, writing prompts is less important in some tools than others. If a tool exists with an automatic prompt and it gets the job done, that might be a good alternative.

How to write good AI prompts

Good prompts include precise instructions and context to steer the AI. Here's how that might look. Let's say I want to find out what are some overarching themes in five somewhat related episodes from my podcast.

So I upload the podcast episodes into Otter to get them transcribed.

From there I'll export the txt file of the transcripts, upload them into Claude and ask:

- These are five different podcast episodes. Could you identify the two most common themes that they all discuss, please.
- <AI responds>
- Great. Thanks. Now please tell me what each podcast guest (or speaker) said about each of those themes.

From there you can decide what to do with that information, which could include:

- Creating quote graphics for social media
- Including the content in an article that discusses the themes

The trick so to speak to writing good AI prompts is to know what you are after. To get good results, you need to be specific, detailed and clear. More is often better.

Use Cases and Benefits of Good AI Prompts

Using AI for some tasks can help us be better content strategists and marketers, but don't lose that personal touch. Like, I've used AI for some ideation and even initial drafting for this article. But by the time it's all set and done, I've updated, deleted and added my own thoughts. Regardless, AI is great for ideation and shortcutting some traditionally longer processes.

Ideation Assistance

AI can give us ideas for article outlines, questions to ask on podcasts and more.

Brand tone

It can help us ensure tone consistency.

Teach the AI how your brand is supposed to sound. Journalist and ghostwriter Bruce Shutan said on "The Business Storytelling

Show" that he uses Otter.ai to transcribe his interviews with brands and then uses that tool to ensure the brand's voice comes through as he writes content for them.

You can also have an ongoing string in tools like Claude AI and ask it to compare a new piece of content against the existing pieces of content from a brand to check tone and style consistency.

Enhanced Creativity

AI can help us be more creative. It's easy to brainstorm for headlines, subject lines and more using AI tools. In some you can even have a conversation:

- Please give me 10 headline ideas for this topic
- OK. Add emojis
- Please make them more witty
- I like this one, can you do xyz

Automate Repurposing

Using proper prompts can help us repurpose content. For example, the prompt sequence to repurpose a blog post could be:

- Please write me 10 LinkedIn posts from this article
- I want to use this blog post as a foundation to an email sent to xyz. Could you spin up a draft please.

From there, follow-ups can make the content better as well and as always ensure to edit the output thoroughly.

Writing targeted, well-structured prompts enables brands to tap into the vast potential of AI for content creation and marketing.

Prompts provide the context, instructions and examples help AI tools to give us better answers which then help us.

The future of AI in your workflow

This is how content creators should look at artificial intelligence in their process: How can it make the process easier while we still create unique and meaningful content? Just asking ChatGPT to write all your blog posts isn't the way to go, and at some point, a lot of content might sound the same if everyone does that.

But maybe at some point, we can teach AI tools our brand voice and style, and it can help us produce content quicker and still ensure that it's unique and will help us stand out.

The key – like it is with any new technology really – is to look at the opportunity and integrate the ones

that make sense to your strategy and
workflows.

One step at a time

Phased Functionality

It used to be that projects were run like this:

Make a plan that includes every single detail.
Once every single detail was ironed out the
implementation would start. Or so much time
has passed that there was enough turnover
in the organization that a new plan had to be
started. Ha.

And then, when the project launched, that
was that. Onto the next project.

Today, things move way too fast in the digital
space to only plan and write plans for months
at a time. There needs to be movement.

Get the minimally working product to market and update it from there based on changes in the marketplace and in user behavior.

Sometimes, we can even uncover user behavior that we previously overlooked.

In a content performance culture, this also applies. We can totally launch a blog strategy without a blog being live.

Start gathering and writing stories. Pieces of them can be shared on social media right now. The full stories can be shared on the blog when it's live.

Many software applications in our lives use this approach, too. Think of all the devices that have software upgrades sent through. Same thing.

Phased functionality can help us get to market quickly (try not to be too quick) and make updates and adjustments live.

When done right, it benefits the organization and the end user.

Content performance cultures get things done. One step at a time, so to speak. And that also means teams keep in mind that it's an ongoing journey.

Let's take the example of building a website and how that's never done.

Launching a website can be an organization's web team's big project for a good amount of time.

Project plans are put into place. Decisions are made on what content management system to use. Roles are defined. Milestones are laid out. People start implementing.

Launching a website does feel like a project because there is a theoretical and actual endpoint to it. That's often the launch of the website. Once it's live, the website re-launch or launch project is done.

And unlike content marketing, social media, or email marketing projects, which can go on forever and ever, website launch project have that finish line – the website launch. Some organizations send out news releases and emails and social media posts announcing the finish line of this digital marketing centerpiece.

It was a lot of work and a lot of effort was put into and it feels like something worth announcing. We reached the goal.

I remember a time years ago even when news media would cover when organizations switched to responsive design even.

But here's the problem with that: launching a website is actually not the finish line in digital marketing or even website strategy. It's just the starting line.

Because the goal is not to actually have a new and better-looking website, but the goal is to have a website that helps us achieve our business goals and helps our customer base. It's the home base of our digital marketing, so to speak. And digital marketing doesn't stop – if you want it to work.

And the way to have a website help our long-term digital marketing goals often includes the following:

- Continuous A/B testing
- Continuous content development to drive search engine optimization and share content audiences actually want to consume.
- Content governance and updates
- Updates based on user behavior changes

I always love hearing from organizations that constantly fiddle with things on their site to test to see what's working and what could be working better and to adjust for I new user behaviors.

That's how digital marketing works. Things change and sometimes they change quickly. So we need to be able to adjust quickly and somewhat on the fly.

And the only way to stay on top of those things is to have a plan for when the website has launched.

So the plan for once the website has launched needs to be in place. And it's not Phase 2 of a website launch but it's actually another phase of the over-arching digital marketing plan.

Of course, there also needs to be a plan for while the website is being developed or updated. Social media is not shutting down and neither should email marketing and even blogging. The time off for activity on all the different relevant digital marketing channels should be kept to a minimum.

How do you integrate a website launch that's fairly extensive with an overall marketing plan? Here's the shell of a timeline without going into all the nitty-gritty details on what's included in launching a website specifically.

Phase 1: Continue doing what you're doing. Digital marketing moves too fast to allow downtime.

Phase 2: Evaluate what's working and what's not working. Do more of what's working and less of what's not working. Make a plan, adjust the current plan or validate what you already have.

Phase 3: Evaluate what content management system you actually need. I'm not going to go into that too deep here because that could be a series of chapters. But many of the systems out there have their advantages and disadvantages, and many of them work and can help you accomplish your goals. Some are expensive and some are cheaper but might take more of your time to implement. Either way, hardly anything is free. You pay one way or another.

Phase 4: Evaluate budget and also in-house expertise. And while some things are commodities, strategy expertise is not one of those things. To a degree, you do get what you pay for.

Phase 5: Pick partners as necessary for all the different phases.

Phase 6a): Have one team focus on building, updating, and re-launching the website.

Phase 6b): Have another team continue with the current digital marketing strategies to ensure there's no gap in digital marketing accomplishments.

Keep in mind that both teams have to continue to talk to each other to ensure everybody's on the same page.

Phase 7: Launch the site and kick up digital marketing into an even higher gear now that the new shiny and well-functional website is up.

Phase 8: Keep going and adjust on the fly based on what works and what doesn't work.

So while building a website is somewhat of a linear project, digital marketing is not as linear as some people would like it to be. Some things can run at the same time and others do build off each other. The key is to not stop and keep adjusting what's working and what's not working.

Using the right tools

Technology tools really should never take center stage. I would recommend this kind of workflow:

- Come up with the strategy first – what are we trying to accomplish?
- Evaluate and update culture – is the culture set up to do what we need to do?
- Pick the tools for the main things you have to accomplish
- Keep re-evaluating

When it comes to software don't get married to a specific vendor but use what works best for you.

The tools aren't changing that we are doing something. They just change the **how** and that how should be easier.

Now, in the often-present case of resisting change – any change – no software tool will ever be perfect.

Some examples of tools that I find necessary:

- A microphone – to voice dictate articles to the computer via Google Docs. An iPhone can do the same trick. AirPods work too.
- Instant messaging – whether it's Slack, Basecamp, Skype, Teams is a choice of preference.
- Video conferencing – yes, Zoom is the best in my opinion, but that doesn't mean others won't work
- Project management – email is not a PM tool. Basecamp, Jira, etc. can do the trick.
- Boomerang and Outlook scheduling. I schedule most of my emails to send at eight in the morning and at one in the afternoon so I cut down on ongoing responses all day.

No matter the tools. they should end up making things easier and fit into a strategy.

As marketing expert Aymar Pirzada reminded us on The Business Storytelling Show "make sure the strategy is written down. Marketers with a documented strategy report more success."

Once the strategy and culture are on the right track, pick a tool. There are many out there and that could be a full time job to continuously evaluate them.

I would recommend verbalizing the top problem you are trying to solve and then go find the most affordable tool for that problem.

If several problems need to be addressed focus on the most pressing ones and find the tool for that first.

Don't get overwhelmed

Good content performance cultures always try new things, but they don't get overwhelmed.

I heard it over the years quite often: I'm trying to catch up. I need to read all those magazines piled up on my desk.

But of course, we don't get to them and when we do, it's in a rush. But trying to catch up feels good and sometimes is an easy excuse.

Another version of this: I need to know all the latest tools and strategies. But, of course it's impossible to know everything and some strategies that work in other industries may not work in yours.

How do we let the internal need to catch up go and move forward? I have some ideas.

Realizing what's holding us back

First of all, like anything in life, we need to realize that it's holding us back. If I constantly feel that having to catch up is a requirement to my success, of course it'll stress me out. No doubt. For example, when I was pitching a lot of speaking engagements I realized that I got to the party too late. I was never ever going to catch up! Until I stopped trying. The goal wasn't to catch up and pitch. The goal was and still is to get picked to speak!

I stopped trying to catch up and made my goal and strategy to pitch at different times.

Finding a Solution

Great content performance cultures find ways to make it work. That can be through updated workflows, technology and even mindsets and prioritization.

Everything should be based on performance. What articles perform and get read the most? Do those first!

What articles seem to drive the most conversions? Those should be up on the priority list as well.

Driving Performance

Creating a performance culture also includes strong strategy practices. We already talked about linking to content but there certainly are other strategies like popups, inline calls to action and even social media.

Other strategies that are important include following best practices - which can be as simple as having readable fonts on a website.

Great content performance cultures bring relevancy to the consumer and get them to take the next step - without constantly interrupting them.

Driving a Content Performance Culture goes beyond creating content - even when it's all great content. If the experience is overly cumbersome it might not perform even if it's good.

Use automation correctly

Automation can really make our lives easier. Why not have

machines do all the mundane and repeatable tasks? Who really wants to do them anyway? Not me, for sure. Plus, machines are probably better at them anyway.

Automation also can present issues. When it's not working and the audience notices. Other times, it's so helpful. For example, I schedule many meetings automagically through Calendly. Until we hop on the phone, I haven't done a thing.

But how much do marketers need to know about specific tools and specific workflows? As is often the answer, the answer likely is: It depends.

Factors at play are:

- team size
- other skills on the team
- difficulty of the tools and products to sell
- budget available for automation tools

The Basics of Common Automation

Automation in content and marketing takes tasks that previously were done by people and now has machines do them.

This can allow teams to focus their time on other potentially, and hopefully higher value tasks.

Sticking with the scheduling meetings via Calendly example. Let's say I attend a conference for 3 days and can take 12 meetings per day – so 36 meetings. If it takes 15 minutes to schedule each just scheduling them takes about 9 hours. Given that there's often a back and forth that can distract from other tasks at hand, it might even take longer because it takes a moment to get in and out of tasks.

Of course, people may say that it's more efficient or better to schedule the meetings themselves. There is some truth to that. One I ran into was at a conference. I used the automatic scheduling and let people pick their spots.

That adds the meeting to their schedule and mine. If I move it, they get the updated invite and also have the option to move it with the click of a button if the new time doesn't work.

The fail happened when I used this function at a huge expo and exhibitors booked meetings that worked for them. I didn't realize I would be running from one huge hall to another basically after every meeting.

I could have fixed that by simply looking at the locations before going and then I could have tried to batch them a bit by location. Or by leaving more walking time in between them - which can easily be set up as an automatic rule in the program.

All those solutions are possible via automation and it's not really a problem of automation versus manual. The real problem was that I didn't think through the complete automation formula.

The mindset that I recommend is: Determine what you're trying to accomplish and then find the automation tool that can get you there the closest. Keep in mind that automation is not perfect either.

Final Thoughts

Content performance cultures understand the importance of diversifying channels and trying to reach the audience everywhere they are and multiple times.

Of course, you only have a content performance culture if you're measuring results toward a stated goal.

But also be realistic: How many people are even in your target audience? If it's 100,000, getting 1 million viewers isn't that helpful.

Ben Smith, publisher of Oldtime Central, explained how many people he expected to have in his overall niche, and then how many were reading content. The numbers were close. Does that mean he has the whole market cornered? Probably not. Some of the readers are likely not exact matches, but are just reading once in a while. Nonetheless, it's a great start.

We cannot or should not compare our own content

creation to a much bigger organization or a much bigger influencer or star or whatever.

Being realistic, spending syndication dollars in a smart way and keep moving forward is often the way to win in content marketing.

Does that mean we have to create a lot of content?

Some experts will continue to tell you that you don't. Just be more deliberate is what they say. I say: Produce the right amount while being deliberate about that.

Many people and companies are now creating so much content. Some of it not very good, sure,

but volume AND volume of good
content matter.